...y Regis, West Midlands in 1962. She read English at Aberystwyth University, then in 1983 became a trainee journalist with the *Birmingham Post and Mail.* She has continued to work in journalism, mainly in a freelance capacity. At first, she specialized in writing about sport, but since 1990 has turned her hand to other subjects, including eating disorders, travel, women's issues and contemporary Christianity.

100 Ways
TO BE AT PEACE

Elizabeth Filleul

Marshall Pickering
An Imprint of HarperCollins*Publishers*

Marshall Pickering is an Imprint of
HarperCollins*Religious*
Part of HarperCollins*Publishers*
77–85 Fulham Palace Road, London W6 8JB

First published in Great Britain
in 1995 by Marshall Pickering

1   3   5   7   9   10   8   6   4   2

Copyright in this compilation © 1995 Elizabeth Filleul

Elizabeth Filleul asserts the moral right to be
identified as the compiler of this work

A catalogue record for this book is
available from the British Library

ISBN 0 557 02966 1

Printed and bound in Great Britain by
Woolnough Bookbinding Limited,
Irthlingborough, Northamptonshire

Introduction

'Nothing gives an author so much pleasure as to find his works respectfully quoted by other ... authors' claimed Benjamin Franklin in *Poor Richard's Almanac*. And judging by the current vogue for anthologies of quotations, there must be thousands of dead – and living! – authors who would be flattered to know that their words of wisdom live on in the age of the 'soundbite'.

100 Ways To Be At Peace is a book of quotations with a difference. It is intended for the Christian who yearns to experience the peace of God in their lives, whatever external struggles they may be having. It is for the Christian who wants to see the peace of God in other people's lives, in their nation and in the world.

But what is peace? According to the *BBC English Dictionary* it is 'a state of undisturbed quiet and calm'. The *Oxford Encyclopaedic English Dictionary* defines it as 'quiet', 'tranquillity', 'mental calm', 'serenity' and 'freedom from or the cessation of war'. As Christians, we recognize that the only true, lasting peace – 'the peace that passes all understanding' – comes from God, and that we shall not experience this lasting peace this side of heaven. But we also recognize that we can experience *glimpses* of that peace here on earth. If we actively seek peace, we shall become more aware of it. Here are some examples of what being at peace can entail:

- Being at peace involves delighting in God's creation – including those creepy-crawlies you don't really like.

- Being at peace is searching for signs of hope in the most dreadful and turbulent situations.

- Being at peace means being reconciled with those who hold a grievance against you or against whom you hold a grievance.

- Being at peace means being aware of other people's good qualities and praising them.

- Being at peace involves a willingness always to learn more about your faith and the world, not thinking that you know all the answers.

- Being at peace is relishing conversations about TV, sport, books and other 'trivia' – not feeling guilty about them.

- Being at peace results from expressing your troubles and griefs and not letting them eat away at you inside.

- Being at peace involves taking risks, for 'the person who never made a mistake never made anything'.

- Being at peace is accepting that God's will for your life is not necessarily the one you've convinced yourself he had planned for you.

- Being at peace is expressing gratitude to God for the family and friends he has given you.

Peace, then, is something we can learn to recognize and grasp. Down the centuries spiritual teachers, writers and leaders, great thinkers, philosophers and psychologists have suggested ways individuals can be at peace. Some of their insights appear in this book. I urge you to read their work, and discover even more strategies for a peaceful life.

The selected quotations show tremendous variety in strategies for being at peace. They cover personal peace, peaceful relationships and world peace. I have my personal favourites; you will too. What will become clear is that there is no one suggestion that is appropriate for every individual at any one time. Much will depend upon your individual personality and your spiritual experiences to date. But there is, I believe, something to help everyone seeking more of the Lord's peace.

Each quotation is accompanied by a suggestion for reflection or practical action. Some suggestions take the form of a question, inviting you to scrutinize those aspects of your personality and lifestyle which may not be conducive to being at peace.

This book is not a 'step-by-step' guide to a peace-filled life. Like anything else in the Christian life, being at peace involves putting in some work. But, by following the advice, you will find yourself thinking more deeply about your life, and how you connect with others, with the world and with God. In the words of Caryl Micklem, editor of *Contemporary Prayers for Public Worship*:

Show us, good Lord,
the peace we should seek,
the peace we must give,
the peace we can give,
the peace we must keep,
the peace we must forgo,
and the peace you have given
in Jesus Christ our Lord.

LET nothing disturb you
Let nothing frighten you
All things pass away:
God never changes.
Patience obtains all things.
He who has God
Finds he lacks nothing;
God alone suffices.

ST TERESA OF AVILA

🐚 Read a newspaper or watch the news on TV and remind yourself that amid all the chaos and troubles of the world, God is constant. The current crises will pass away as others have, but God never changes.

Use helpful images

I had another prayer picture one morning as I lay in bed, worried about going to school. I imagined Jesus coming into my room, standing at the foot of my bed, and winking at me. I smiled and got out of bed. No matter what happened that day, Jesus and I were in it together.

JO IND, *Fat is a Spiritual Issue*

🌰 What images of Jesus help you in your daily life? Use those images as you go through your duties today.

Learn from uncomfortable feelings

THE coming of Jesus Christ is not a peaceful thing, it is overwhelming and frantically disturbing, because the first thing he does is to destroy every peace that is not based on a personal relationship to himself.

OSWALD CHAMBERS, *Shadow of an Agony*

&❧ Which activities which used to make you happy now make you feel uncomfortable? Is it because they are detrimental to your relationship with God?

Take a risk

To laugh is to risk appearing the fool.

To weep is to risk appearing sentimental.

To reach out for another is to risk involvement.

To expose feelings is to risk exposing your true self.

To place your ideas, your dreams, before a crowd is to risk their loss.

To love is to risk not being loved in return.

To live is to risk dying.

To hope is to risk despair.

To try is to risk failure.

But risks must be taken, for the greater hazard is to risk nothing.

The person who risks nothing, does nothing, has nothing and is nothing.

They may avoid suffering and sorrow, but they cannot learn, change, grow, love, live.

Chained by their attitude, they are a slave, they have forfeited freedom.

Only a person who risks is free.

ANONYMOUS

☙ Risk doing something you've long been afraid to do, then reflect on the outcome.

NEXT to theology I give to music the highest place and honour. Music is the art of the prophets, the only sound that can calm the agitations of the soul; it is one of the most magnificent and delightful presents God has given us.

MARTIN LUTHER

🎵 Play one of your favourite pieces of music. Praise God for the talent he gave to the composer and musicians. Consider using music more often in your daily reflections.

Don't exclude yourself

DON'T exclude yourself ...
from precious moments
warm encounters
beautiful attitudes
majestic discoveries
flowing intimacies
sensory developments
for these are jewels placed
in the crown of your destiny.
WALTER RINDER

❧ Don't exclude yourself from anything God has to offer you. Be open to new experiences, ideas and sensations.

O God, our Father, there are things today which make us ashamed when we remember them.

Forgive us if we have lost our temper with the people who get on our nerves.

Forgive us if we have been cross and irritable with those who are nearest and dearest to us.

Forgive us if at any time we were discourteous and impolite to those with whom we came into contact in our work.

Forgive us if we have thoughtlessly or deliberately hurt anyone's feelings today.

WILLIAM BARCLAY, *The Plain Man's Book of Prayers*

Say this prayer tonight, before you go to sleep. Then behave towards other people in a way which prevents you from having to pray it again tomorrow.

Be weak

COME in weakness; find strength.
Come in sickness; find health.
Come in confusion; find peace.
Come in sorrow; find joy.
Come in doubt; find faith.
Come in despair; find courage.

Come unready;
Come alone;
Find Christ.
More Contemporary Prayers, edited by Caryl Micklem

🙞 Remember that however weak you feel your
physical or emotional state may be, God can
strengthen you. Depend on him.

O N that day, when evening had come, he said to them, 'Let us go across to the other side.' And leaving the crowd behind, they took him with them in the boat, just as he was. Other boats were with him. A great windstorm arose, and the waves beat into the boat, so that the boat was already being swamped. But he was in the stern, asleep on a cushion; and they woke him up and said to him, 'Teacher, do you not care that we are perishing?'

He woke up and rebuked the wind and said to the sea, 'Peace! Be still!' Then the wind ceased, and there was a dead calm. He said to them, 'Why are you afraid? Have you still no faith?'

And they were filled with great awe and said to one another, 'Who then is this, that even the wind and the sea obey him?'

MARK 4:35–41

🐟 Marvel at the power Jesus showed in stilling the storm. If he is on your side, what chance does anyone have against you?

Celebrate a new year

IT doesn't take a new year
To begin our lives anew –
God grants us new beginnings
Each day the whole year through,
So never be discouraged
For there comes daily to all men
The chance to make another start
And begin all over again!
HELEN STEINER RICE

🐾 Celebrate a personal new year today. Resolve to
make a fresh start with God. Let this truly be the first
day of the rest of your life.

PEACE of mind
comes from not wanting
to change others,
but by simply accepting them
as they are.

True acceptance
is always without demands
and expectations.

GERALD G. JAMPOLSKY, *Letting Go of Fear*

🐾 Stop nagging another person to drop a habit which
irritates you. Simply love them for who they are and
feel the petty tensions melt away.

Don't be afraid

GOD, help us to live slowly;
To move simply;
To look softly;
To allow emptiness;
To let the heart create for us.
Amen.

MICHAEL LEUNIG, *Common Prayer Collection*

🍃 Don't be afraid of any feelings—whether sad,
empty or lonely. Our feelings make us *living* creatures.
Celebrate all aspects of your life—both light and dark.

KEEP thyself first in peace, and then thou shalt be able to pacify others. A peaceable man does more good than he that is well learned.

THOMAS À KEMPIS, *The Imitation of Christ*

🔔 How peaceful a person are you? Pray for peace in your own heart and strive to live a peaceful life.

Pray for world peace

GOD our Father, creator of the world,
please help us to love one another.
Make nations friendly with other nations;
make all of us love one another like brothers and sisters.
Help us to do our part to bring peace in the world
and happiness to all people.
JAPANESE PRAYER

❧ Join or form a prayer group to pray for
world peace.

WHO can boast of being free?
Who has not got secret prisons,
invisible chains, all the more constricting
the less they are apparent?

DOM HELDER CAMERA

🍂 What 'secret prison' are you chained in? Confess it
to a trusted friend. Pray together for your 'release'.

Enjoy trivia

So much of my time is spent in needless hurry;
in saying 'Excuse me; can't stop, sorry,
—so much to do; must rush.'
The joy of casual conversation is cut short,
because somehow I think chatting is merely wasting
     time.
My efficiency robs me of pleasure.
Lord, teach me that time spent talking
of books, of sport, of last night's television
is not time lost, but time enriched.
FRANK TOPPING

  Spend some time today enjoying a casual
conversation about last night's TV, sport,
books or another interest.

GRATITUDE
helps you to grow and expand;
gratitude brings joy
and laughter into your lives
and the lives of all those
around you.

EILEEN CADDY, *The Dawn of Change*

🍃 Write a 'thank you for being you' letter to someone who means a lot to you, or invite them round
for dinner and express your gratitude in a more
direct way.

Learn from failure

WE learn wisdom from failure
much more than from success;
We often discover what will do,
by finding out what will not do;
and probably he who never made a mistake
never made a discovery.
SAMUEL SMILES

❧ Think back to the last time you failed at something
important to you—make a list of the things you
learned from the experience. Share your insights
with anyone you know who is currently
experiencing failure.

See God as your true peace

THUS I saw God to be our true peace, who keeps us safe when we are anything but peaceful, and who always works to bring us to everlasting peace.

ST JULIAN OF NORWICH,
Revelations of Divine Love

🕭 Thank God for bringing you true peace, and try to relish it as often as you can.

Use your 'natural breaks'

IN the rush and noise of life, as you have intervals, step inside yourselves and be still. Wait upon God and feel his good presence; this will carry you through the day's business.

WILLIAM PENN

🐾 Resolve to make use of 'natural breaks' in your daily schedule by spending time with God.

Don't yearn for wealth or power

REAL joy and peace do not depend on power, kingly wealth or other material possessions. If this were so, all people of wealth in the world would be happy and contented, and princes like Buddha, Mahavira and Bhartari would not have renounced their kingdom. But this real and permanent joy is found only in the kingdom of God, which is established in the heart when we are born again.

SADHU SUNDAR SINGH, *With and Without Christ*

🌿 Think of people in the public eye who are very wealthy or powerful. Do they seem to lead happy, problem-free lives? Praise God that the only true contentment comes from knowing him, and that that is something which we can all do.

Praise other people

TAKE an active part in the praising of others, entertaining their good with delight. In no way should you give in to the desire to disparage them, or lessen their praise, or make any objection. You should never think that hearing the good report of another in any way lessens your worth .... Be content when you see or hear that others are doing well in their jobs and with their income, even when you are not. In the same manner, be content when someone else's work is approved and yours is rejected.

JEREMY TAYLOR,
The Rule and Exercises of Holy Living

🐾 Today, praise another person for a quality they have that you have never mentioned before.

THEREFORE, remember, do not look to others or to the reasoning of the wise, but keep yourself where you have felt the Lord visit you that he may visit you again and again – every day – teaching you more and more the way to his dwelling place, drawing you near to the place where there is righteousness, life, rest and peace – forever!

ISAAC PENINGTON, *Letters on Spiritual Values*

At what times and in what places have you felt God's presence? Is there a special place and time when you meet with God? Return to it again and again.

Be aware of God's wonders

No great works and wonders God has ever wrought or shall ever do in or through his created world, not even God himself in his goodness, will make me blessed if they remain outside of me. For blessedness is only present to the extent to which it is within me, as a happening, as an inner knowledge, as love, as feeling, as taste.

THEOLOGICA GERMANICA

🐾 Think of ways to be more personally aware of God's works and wonders. Ask other people for suggestions.

WHAT concerns me still is that many Christians have
not discerned that God made only one John Wimber
and one Graham Kendrick; that this same God created
each of us to play faithfully our note without which the
great symphony of life will be incomplete.

JOYCE HUGGETT, *Finding Freedom*

🔖 Is there a church leader – well-known or other-
wise – that you try to emulate? Stop, and be
yourself – you have just as much to offer.

Recognize the fruits of obedience

[ABIJAH's son] Asa succeeded him. In his days the land had rest for ten years. Asa did what was good and right in the eyes of the Lord his God. He took away the foreign altars and the high places, broke down the pillars, hewed down the sacred poles, and commanded Judah to seek the Lord, the God of their ancestors, and to keep the law and the commandment. He also removed from all the cities of Judah the high places and the incense altars. And the kingdom had rest under him. He built fortified cities in Judah while the land had rest. He had no war in those years, for the Lord gave him peace.

2 CHRONICLES 14:1-6

🐾 What difference do you think it would make to the world if its leaders obeyed God's word? Pray for your country's leaders.

Always be willing to learn

LORD Jesus, I don't know much about you,
But I am willing to learn,
And I am ready to give all that I know of myself
To all that I know of you;
And I am willing to go on learning.

DONALD COGGAN

🔖 Buy or borrow a book or some daily study notes
about Jesus which you've never read before. Inform
yourself and resolve to continue your studying
in the directions which capture your interest.

Meditate on Christ

MOST merciful Lord,
turn my lukewarmness into a fervent love of you.
Most gentle Lord,
my prayer tends towards this –
that by remembering and meditating
on the good things you have done
I may be enkindled with your love.

ST ANSELM, *Prayers and Meditations*

🍂 Select a passage about Jesus' earthly ministry from
one of the gospels and meditate on it. What does the
passage tell you about Jesus? How can you translate
the lesson into your own life?

IF I can stop one heart from breaking,
I shall not live in vain;
If I can ease one life the aching,
Or cool one pain,
Or help one fainting robin
Unto his nest again,
I shall not live in vain.

EMILY DICKINSON

🐾 Go out of your way to help someone
or something else today.

Cherish all spiritual experiences

THE day had been rich but strenuous so I climbed Signal Hill back of my house talking and listening to God all the way up, all the way back, all the lovely half hour on the top. And God talked back! I let my tongue go loose and from it there flowed poetry far more beautiful than any I ever composed. It flowed without pausing and without ever a failing syllable for a half hour. I listened astonished and full of joy and gratitude. I wanted a Dictaphone for I knew that I should not be able to remember it – and now I cannot. 'Why', someone may ask, 'did God waste his poetry on you alone, when you could not carry it home?' You will have to ask God that question. I only know that he did and I am happy in the memory.

FRANK LAUBACH, *Letters by a Modern Mystic*

❦ Have you ever had a spiritual experience that has received a cynical response from other people? Have you ever felt sceptical about another Christian's experiences? Just accept your own and be happy in them – and be grateful that God communes with others, even though you cannot always understand his ways.

OUR sin is against the Living Order, and we have neither inward peace nor inward power until we have offered prayers of penitence. Confession, like thanksgiving, should be specific. It should not be ruthless, but it should not excuse: it should set hooks into the facts. 'I confess *this* sharp judgement, *this* jealousy, *this* cowardice, *this* bondage of dark habit, *this* part in the world's evil.'

GEORGE A. BUTTRICK, *Prayer*

🐾 Confess your sins, naming them specifically, to God. Then ask for forgiveness and start again with a 'clean sheet'.

Be transformed

JUST as a little drop of water mixed with a lot of wine seems to entirely lose its own identity as it takes on the taste and colour of the wine; just as iron, heated and glowing, looks very much like fire, having lost its original appearance; just as air flooded with the light of the sun is transformed into the same splendour of the light so that it appears to be light itself, so it is like for those who melt away from themselves and are entirely transfused into the will of God.

BERNARD OF CLAIRVAUX, *On the Love of God*

❧ Look back over your life since you became a Christian. In which ways have you been 'transfused into the will of God'? Thank God for the changes he has made in your life. Be prepared to embrace any more such changes in the future.

ALWAYS remember to forget
The troubles that passed away
But never forget to remember
The blessings that come every day.

ANONYMOUS

❧ Resolve not to brood on past problems, but to be
thankful for the daily blessings you receive.

Be spontaneous

G O D bless our contradictions, those parts of us which seem to be out of character. Let us be creatures of paradox and variety; creatures of contrast; of light and shade; creatures of faith. God be our constant. Let us step out of character into the unknown, to struggle and love and do what we will. Amen.

MICHAEL LEUNIG, *Common Prayer Collection*

🌰 Follow an impulse today, and relish being out of character.

Y O U may either win your peace or buy it; win it, by resistance to evil; buy it, by compromise with evil.

JOHN RUSKIN

❧ Think about times when peace has been won by resistance to evil – e.g. during World War Two. Pray for those who challenge evil today. Practise this same resistance in your own daily encounters.

Pray the 'serenity prayer'

LORD, grant me the serenity to accept the things I cannot change, courage to change the things I can, and wisdom to know the difference.

REINHOLD NIEBUHR

🍂 Write this prayer in your Bible or in another prominent place and make it your own.

RESTFULNESS, though, is a form of awareness, a way of being in life. It is being in ordinary life with a sense of ease, gratitude, appreciation, peace and prayer. We are restful when ordinary life is enough.

RONALD ROLHEISER, *The Shattered Lantern*

🦋 Let ordinary life be enough for you today. Feel contented and restful rather than frustrated and restless. Enjoy the peace.

Live a balanced life

PEACE comes from living a measured life. Peace comes from attending to every part of my world in a sacramental way. My relationships are not what I do when I have time left over from my work .... Reading is not something I do when life calms down. Prayer is not something I do when I feel like it. They are all channels of hope and growth for me. They must all be given their due.

JOAN D. CHITTESTER

🐚 Which activities have you been neglecting lately? Make some time for one of them today and resolve to juggle your time to take part in it more regularly.

Do something you should do

HOW often have I found out that we grow to maturity not by doing what we like, but by doing what we should? How true it is that not every *should* is a compulsion, and not every *like* is a high morality and true freedom.

KARL RAHNER

🔖 Think of one thing you really *should* do that you've been putting off – and do it today.

Desire nothing

To reach satisfaction in all
desire its possession in nothing.
To come to possess all
desire the possession of nothing.
To arrive at being all
desire to be nothing.
To come to the knowledge of all
desire the knowledge of nothing ...
Because if you desire to have something in all
your treasure in God is purely your all.

St John of the Cross

For today, forget about all the ambitions and hopes
you have and concentrate on God alone.

Do whatever you can

I T is the greatest
of all mistakes
to do nothing because you
can only do a little.
Do what you can.

SYDNEY SMITH

🐚 Do whatever you can to make a difference to some
injustice in the world, in your work, in your church, or
in your relationships.

Choose the lower places in life

FINALLY, I want to teach you the way of true peace and true liberty. There are four things you must do. First, strive to do another's will rather than your own. Second, choose always to have less than more. Third, seek the lower places in life, dying to the need to be recognized and important. Fourth, always and in everything desire that the will of God may be completely fulfilled in you. The person who tries this will be treading the frontiers of peace and rest.

THOMAS À KEMPIS, *The Imitation of Christ*

🐾 Try Thomas à Kempis' advice for yourself over the next few days. Reflect on the outcome.

WHEN you feel
that you have reached the end
and that you cannot go
one step further,
when life seems to be
drained of all purpose:
What a wonderful opportunity
to start all over again
to turn over a new page.

EILEEN CADDY, *Footprints on the Path*

❧ Imagine the rest of your life is an empty page. How
would you want to fill it? What changes would you
make from the life you are leading now? Talk
to God about the changes you would make,
the new beginning you would like. Ask him to
help you start afresh.

Concentrate on the present

IT is no use to pray for the old days; stand square where you are and make the present better than the past has been.

OSWALD CHAMBERS, *Shade of His Hand*

🎋 Identify mistakes of the past which still trouble you or recur. How can you ensure they don't continue to do so? Ask God to help you make your present better than your past.

Pray against superficiality

SUPERFICIALITY is the curse of our age. The doctrine of constant satisfaction is a primary spiritual problem. The desperate need today is not for a greater number of intelligent people, or gifted people, but for deep people.

RICHARD FOSTER, *A Celebration of Discipline*

🐚 Is there evidence of superficiality in your own life? If so, pray about it, and about the prevalence of superficiality throughout society.

Notice signs of hope

LORD, make me a child of hope, reborn from apathy, cynicism and despair, ready to work for that new man you have made possible by walking the way of the cross yourself.

I do have hope grounded on your victory over powers of evil, death itself; focused on your kingdom, breaking on us now as light out of deep darkness.

And I do see signs of hope immediately around me. I see a wider sign: I see a sign – flowers growing on a bombed-out site. The sign – an empty cross. The burden, Lord, is yours.

Lord, I am a prisoner of hope! There is life before death.

NORTHERN IRELAND PRAYER

🦐 Be alert for signs of hope in the most tragic situation you encounter (either personally or in the media) today.

S o when you are offering your gift at the altar, if you remember that your brother or sister has something against you, leave your gift there before the altar and go; first be reconciled with your brother or sister, and then come and offer your gift.

MATTHEW 5:23–4

🔖 Is there anyone who, right now, is nursing a grievance against you? Before doing anything else, make peace with them.

Use time wisely

LORD, I have time,
I have plenty of time,
All the time that you give me,
The years of my life,
The days of my years,
The hours of my days,
They are all mine.
Mine to fill, quietly, calmly,
But to fill completely, up to the brim,
To offer them to you, that of their insipid water
You may make a rich wine such as you made once in
Cana of Galilee.
MICHEL QUOIST

• How, ideally, would you like to fill the next few
hours for God? Set aside some time to do those
very things.

THE peace of God be with you,
The peace of Christ be with you,
The peace of the Spirit be with you,
And with your children,
From the day that we have here today
To the day of the end of your lives,
Until the day of the end of your lives.

CELTIC PRAYER

🐾 Ask God's blessing on a neighbour or
colleague today.

Don't let hurts dominate your life

THIS is what resurrection LIFE is about; not being immune to pain, injustice, betrayals, helplessness, but not letting them dominate.

DELIA SMITH, *A Journey into God*

🐝 When troubles or illness come along, do you find they occupy your every waking hour? Ask God to strengthen you for future problems, so that they do not dominate your life and hinder your relationship with him.

Practise forgiveness

You will know no peace until you discover how to forgive yourself, to forgive other people and to let others forgive you.

DOROTHY ROWE

Forgive yourself completely for something you feel you've done wrong. Then forget about it and move on.

Praise the God of creation

H E is the living God, that clothes the earth with grass and herbs, causes the trees to grow and bring forth food for you, and makes the fishes of the sea to breathe and live. He makes the fowls of the air to breed and causes the buck and the doe, the creatures, and all the beasts, to bring forth whereby they may be food for you. He is the living God, that causes the sun to give warmth to you, to nourish you when you are cold. He is the living God, that causes the snow and frost to melt and causes the rain to water the plants. He is the living God, that made heaven and earth, the clouds, causes the springs to break out of the rocks, and divided the great sea from the earth. He divides the light from the darkness, by which it is called day and the darkness night, and divided the great waters from the earth, gathered them together, which great waters he called sea and the dry land earth. He is to be worshipped that does this. He is the living God that gives you breath, life and strength and gives you beasts and cattle whereby you may be fed and clothed. He is the living God and he is to be worshipped.

GEORGE FOX, *Letters*

🐾 Look out of your window and praise God for all you see around you that he has created. Strive to do this as often as you can.

DEEP peace pure white
of the moon to you.
Deep peace pure green
of the grass to you.
Deep peace pure brown
of the earth to you.
Deep peace pure grey
of the dew to you.
Deep peace pure blue
of the sky to you.

FIONA MACLEOD

❧ Notice the deep, beautiful colours of all you see today. Praise God for such infinite variety and subtlety, and for the fact that you can see and appreciate it.

Spend time in silence

G o placidly amid the noise and the haste and remember what peace there may be in silence.
MAX EHRMANN

❧ How long has it been since you last sat quietly on your own with God? Set aside some time to spend in silence this week.

Pray about a trouble spot

O God of many names,
lover of all nations,
we pray for peace
in our hearts,
in our homes,
in our nations,
in our world,
the peace of your will,
the peace of our need.

BISHOP GEORGE APPLETON

Choose a world trouble spot and resolve to pray
for it daily. Pray too about any discord in your own
home or work life.

Look forward

THE worst thing
you can possibly do
is worry about
what you could have done.
LICHENBURG

🏵 Resolve never to think of what might have been if
you'd done something else. Look forward, not back.

Don't take life for granted

BLESSED are those who do not take life for granted,
   for they are within measurable distance of taking it
   as granted them by God.
Blessed are those who learn to see the finger of God in
   the conspiracy of accidents that make up their lives,
   they shall be rewarded with daily miracles.
Blessed are those who say yes to something higher
   than themselves, in that genuflection they will say
   the creed.
Blessed are those who take on the heart of a child and
   the heart of a virgin, they shall again delight in Santa
   and believe in God.
Blessed are those whose discipleship includes the
   discipline of regular prayer, they shall know that it is
   in God that they live and move and have their being.
Blessed are those who kiss a leper, who make
   preferential option for the poor, for love and God
   will overwhelm them.
Blessed are those who make this a lifelong quest, they
   will make a good beginning.

RONALD ROLHEISER, *The Shattered Lantern*

   ❧ Praise God for the life he has given you,
   and do this every day.

Be submissive to God

FOR when the soul is tossed and troubled and alone in its unrest, it is time to pray so as to make itself sensitive and submissive to God.
ST JULIAN OF NORWICH,
Revelations of Divine Love

🐾 Check that what you are doing with your life is in line with what God wants you to do. Continue to pray and listen to what God is telling you.

Look for the light

ALL the darkness of the world cannot put out the
light of one small candle.

ANONYMOUS

🍃 Think of people or organizations who act as 'small
candles' in dark or turbulent areas of the world. Pray
for and thank God for them. Consider what light *you*
can shed in the world.

Relax!

HE will not let your foot be moved,
he who keeps you will not slumber.
He who keeps Israel
will neither slumber nor sleep.
PSALM 121:3–4

🔊 Take a rest from your duties and concerns for a
while, knowing that God is never asleep and constantly
watches over you.

Gᴏᴅ's main concern is that we are more interested in him than in work for him. Once you are rooted and grounded in Christ the great thing you can do is to *be*. Don't try and be useful; be yourself and God will use you to further his ends.

Oꜱᴡᴀʟᴅ Cʜᴀᴍʙᴇʀꜱ, *Approved Unto God*

🔖 Stop thinking about what you can do for God and just concentrate on getting to know him better. He will use you in his own time and his own way.

Explore alternatives

PEOPLE who feel they have to do things usually
forfeit many available options and alternatives and lose
control of their lives in the process.
DENIS WAITLEY

❧ Take a fresh look at your current plans for your life.
In pursuing them so rigidly, might you be missing out
on other, better options God has in mind for you?

LEAD me from death
to life, from falsehood to truth

Lead me from despair
to hope, from fear to trust

Lead me from hate
to love, from war to peace

Let peace fill our heart,
our world, our universe.

SATISH KUMAR

🍂 Pray this prayer for yourself first and then for your
nation today.

Don't rely on feelings

FOR the truth is the feelings we receive from our devotional life are the least of its benefits. The invisible and unfelt grace of God is much greater, and it is beyond our comprehension.

ST JOHN OF THE CROSS,
The Dark Night of the Soul

• This week, try not to judge your spiritual life on how you feel. Accept that God is with you and working through you, even though you may not be aware of his presence.

HAVE no fear
of moving into the unknown.
Simply step out fearlessly
knowing that I am with you,
therefore no harm can befall you;
all is very well.

EILEEN CADDY, *Footprints on the Path*

🦢 Today do something you have been putting off
through lack of confidence or fear, knowing
that God is with you.

Look for life's 'little advantages'

HUMAN felicity is produced not so much by great pieces of good fortune that seldom happen as by little advantages that occur every day.

BENJAMIN FRANKLIN

🐚 Today, look for the 'little advantages' that occur in your life and thank God for them.

I T is enough to be, in an ordinary human mode, with one's hunger and sleep, one's cold and warmth, rising and going to bed. Putting on blankets and taking them off, making coffee and then drinking it. Defrosting the refrigerator, reading, meditating, working, praying. I live as my fathers have lived on this earth, until eventually I die.

THOMAS MERTON

🦢 Today, as you carry out your ordinary activities, thank God for them and really enjoy them. Remember that meaning, purpose and peace may be found in simple, ordinary things.

Enjoy God's gifts

WE thank you, Father, for all there is to enjoy:
the beauty of land and sea and sky;
the companionship of pets and the fascination of wild
    life;
the society of other people – conversation, dancing,
    games and exercise; the wit and wisdom of men;
crafts and hobbies, literature, music, painting, plays
    and films;
the pleasures of recollection and the excitement of
    looking forward;
the services of the church; the life of the spirit here and
    now and the hope of the full life to come.
For all these things, we thank you, Lord, and ask that
    all people shall have their chance to enjoy them.
More Contemporary Prayers, edited by Caryl Micklem

🐾 Today, enjoy one of the pleasures mentioned above
– go dancing or to a play, walk your dog, spend time
chatting with a friend. Think on the experience and
thank God for it at the end of the day.

THEREFORE I tell you, do not worry about your life, what you will eat, or about your body, what you will wear. For life is more than food, and the body more than clothing. Consider the ravens: they neither sow nor reap, they have neither storehouse nor barn, and yet God feeds them. Of much more value are you than the birds! And can any of you by worrying add a single hour to your span of life? If then you are not able to do so small a thing as that, why do you worry about the rest? Consider the lilies, how they grow: they neither toil nor spin; yet I tell you, even Solomon in all his glory was not clothed like one of these. But if God so clothes the grass of the field, which is alive today and tomorrow is thrown into the oven, how much more will he clothe you – you of little faith! And do not keep striving for what you are to eat and what you are to drink, and do not keep worrying. For it is the nations of the world that strive after all these things, and your Father knows that you need them. Instead, strive for his kingdom, and these things will be given to you as well.

LUKE 12:22–31

🍃 Today, forget any worries you may have about your weight, diet or clothing.

Pray about everything

WHAT a friend we have in Jesus
All our sins and griefs to bear!
What a privilege to carry
Everything to God in prayer!
O what peace we often forfeit,
O what needless pain we bear,
All because we do not carry
Everything to God in prayer.
JOSEPH MEDICOTT SCRIVEN

❧ Bring one of your deepest concerns before the
Lord. Then try to forget it for one day, leaving it in
God's hands.

Do something at once

YOU can't do everything at once – but you can do
something at once.

ANONYMOUS

    🐾 Make a start – however small – on one of your
outstanding tasks. Even a little step will be a positive
move towards completing it.

Know that God has always loved you

FOR it was you who formed my inward parts;
you knit me together in my mother's womb.
I praise you, for I am fearfully and wonderfully made.
Wonderful are your works;
that I know very well.
My frame was not hidden from you,
when I was being made in secret,
intricately woven in the depths of the earth.
Your eyes beheld my unformed substance.
In your book were written
all the days that were formed for me
when none of them as yet existed.
PSALM 139:13–16

🍃 Thank God that he cared for you and had plans for
you even before you were born.

Don't worry about what might not happen

SOME of your hurts you have cured,
And the sharpest you still have survived,
But what torments of grief you endured
From evils which never arrived!

RALPH WALDO EMERSON

When next you find yourself worrying about
something which might not happen, banish the
worry from your mind. Remember, everything
is in God's hands.

Find your vocation

FIND inner peace and you will
have endless energy –
the more you give,
the more you receive.
After you have found
your calling
you work easily
and joyously.
You never get tired.
PEACE PILGRIM

❧ What job do you think God really wants you to do?
Try to discern this through prayer.

Make the most of what you have

WHY do we seek profit? What did Judas profit for being with Christ? Or what profit was the law to the Jews? Or paradise to Adam? Or the promised land to the Israelites? We should keep our mind fixed on one point only: how we may do what is best with the resources we have been given.

JOHN CHRYSOSTOM, *Dead to Sin*

🐾 Take a fresh look at your resources – your talents, skills, finances. Are you making the most of them?

Play your tune!

THE same breath is blown into the flute, cornet and bagpipe, but different music is produced according to the different instruments. In the same way the one Spirit works in us, God's children, but different results are produced, and God is glorified through them according to each one's temperament and personality.

SADHU SUNDAR SINGH, *With and Without Christ*

🍂 What kind of 'music' do you play for the Lord? Think about the 'music' produced by other Christians you know – and how all work together as one.

PATIENCE is necessary in this life, because so much of life is fraught with adversity. No matter how hard we try, our lives will never be without strife and grief. Thus, we should not strive for a peace that is without temptation, or for a life that never feels adversity. Peace is not found by escaping temptations, but by being tried by them. We will have discovered peace when we have been tried and come through the trial of temptation.

THOMAS À KEMPIS, *The Imitation of Christ*

❧ Look back on times of adversity, and remember the lessons you learned and the blessings that transpired. Send flowers and a message of support to a friend who you know is going through a bad time.

Be inefficient

THOMAS Merton was once asked by a journalist what he considered to be one of the leading spiritual diseases of our time .... Of all the things he might have suggested (lack of prayer, lack of community, poor morals, lack of concern for justice and the poor) he answered instead with one word, efficiency. Why? Because, he continued, 'from the monastery to the Pentagon, the plant has to run ... and there is little time or energy left over after that to do anything else.' What Merton is pointing out here is that, regarding God and religion, our problem is not so much badness as it is busyness.

ROLAND ROLHEISER, *The Shattered Lantern*

❧ This week, set aside one day (preferably a non-work day!) where you can be completely inefficient. Instead of completing an outstanding task, just spend the day focusing on God.

Learn from the 'insignificant'

AND he showed me more, a little thing, the size of a hazelnut, on the palm of my hand, round like a ball. I looked at it thoughtfully and wondered, 'What is this?'

And the answer came, 'It is all that is made.' I marvelled that it continued to exist and did not suddenly disintegrate; it was so small. And again my mind supplied the answer, 'It exists, both now and forever, because God loves it.'

ST JULIAN OF NORWICH,
Revelations of Divine Love

🐚 Pick up something small – e.g. a leaf, a conker, a flower – from your garden or the local park. Examine it closely and marvel that God loves and cares for something so small and apparently meaningless. If it exists because God loves it, what does that say about you?

Don't say too much

HE that would live in peace and ease
Must not speak all he knows nor judge all he sees.
BENJAMIN FRANKLIN

❦ Remember that opinions often lead to conflict.
Ask God to help you to discern when it is best to
stay silent.

Look upward

I avoid looking forward or backward,
And try to keep looking *upward*.

CHARLOTTE BRONTË

🦋 When next you find yourself remembering the past
or focusing on the possible future, talk to God instead.

Believe

I do not seek to understand so that I may believe,
but I believe so that I may understand;
and what is more,
I believe that unless I do believe I shall not understand.
ST ANSELM, *Prayers and Meditations*

❧ Accept the promises of the Bible in faith even
though you do not always understand them.

Know that God is all-suffering

SOMEWHERE, beneath the shock and anger, was the realization that God was not macho. He was not all-glorious above without being all-suffering below. God was Jesus who wept when Lazarus died. God was Jesus who sweated drops of blood. God was Jesus who ached and suffered and bled and died. God was not so much sorry as stuck right in there, starving to death in Cairo, dying in Dave, smashed in the jar. It was not a matter of God versus us or vice versa. It was God in us – God in the midst of our suffering as he died on the cross, us in the midst of God's suffering as we ached deep inside us.

JO IND, *Fat is a Spiritual Issue*

🍃 Look at pictures of suffering people in the news today. Think of God suffering with them: in that earthquake, famine, prison camp, war.

Don't wait for perfection

NOTHING would be done at all
if a man waited
until he could do it so well
that no one could find
fault with it.
CARDINAL NEWMAN

🍂 What are you putting off doing until you can do it
very well? Take the plunge and do it straight away.

WHEN I'm confused, Lord, show me the way,
show me, show me the way.
Baffled and bruised, Lord, show me the way,
show me, show me the way.
Still my heart and clear my mind,
prepare my soul to hear
your still, small voice, your word of truth:
'Peace, be still, your Lord is near.
Always so close to show you the way,
show you, show you the way.'

WENDY CRAIG

❧ Ask God to guide mentally and emotionally, as well
as spiritually and physically. Thank him for his
guidance in the past.

Express your troubles

O Jesus, what a trouble it is to have to strive against the opinions of so many people! When I thought it was all settled, it all began again, for it was not enough to give them what they asked, they at once found some fresh obstacle. When I write of it like this it seems nothing, but it was very hard to endure.

St Teresa of Avila

🦋 Write, draw or talk any frustrations out of your system.

A man should therefore place such complete trust in God, that he has no need of comfort from men. When a good man is troubled, tempted, or vexed by evil thoughts, he comes more clearly than ever to realize his need of God, without whom he can do nothing good. Then, as he grieves and laments his lot, he turns to money amid his misfortunes. He is weary of life, and longs for death to release him, that he may be dissolved and be with Christ. It is then that he knows with certainty that there can be no complete security nor perfect peace in his life.

THOMAS À KEMPIS, *The Imitation of Christ*

Stop fishing for human compliments and turn to God for affirmation.

Appreciate all creatures

GOD, this is your world,
you made us, you love us;
teach us how to live in the world that you have made.
HOPE FREEMAN

🦋 Think of a creature God has made which you
dislike or are afraid of. Read a book about them, to
discover how other creatures are dependent upon
them. Praise God for his intricate, perfect structure
and acknowledge that you are only one, small part
of life.

G O D is nice. And he likes me.

ADRIAN PLASS,
The Growing Up Pains of Adrian Plass

🐾 Do you see God as someone who is nice and who
likes you, whatever your faults? If you have trouble
with this, ask him to help you see him as a loving
father and friend.

Be happy!

HE that thinks himself the happiest man alive really is so.

C. C. COLTON

❧ Think of all the things in your life which make you happy – and be contented with them.

DROP thy still dews of quietness
Till all our strivings cease
Take from our souls the strain and stress
And let our ordered lives confess
The beauty of thy peace.

J. G. WHITHER

Ask God to take away your current stresses, and just relax in his peace.

See God in everything

GOD can be very present within an event, but we can be so self-preoccupied and focused upon our headaches, heartaches, tasks, daydreams, and restless distractions that we can be oblivious to that presence.
RONALD ROLHEISER, *The Shattered Lantern*

🥢 Whatever you do today, look for God's presence in your life.

LIVE
as you will have
wished to have lived
when you are dying.

C. F. GELLERT

If you were told today that you had three months
to live, what three things would you most like to
accomplish or complete in that time? Write them
down and in the next three months, try to do them.

Know your faith is from God

FOR some time ago Theudas rose up, claiming to be somebody and a number of men, about four hundred, joined him; but he was killed, and all who followed him were dispersed and disappeared. After him Judas the Galilean rose up at the time of the census and got people to follow him; he also perished, and all who followed him were scattered. So in the present case, I tell you, keep away from these men and let them alone; because if this plan or this understanding is of human origin, it will fail, but if it is of God, you will not be able to overthrow them – in that case you may even be found fighting against God!

ACTS 5:36-9

ᔋ Think of religions and ideologies which have come and gone. Would Christianity have survived so long if it were not the truth? Relax in your faith, and thank God for showing you the truth.

We would enjoy much peace if we did not busy ourselves with what other people say and do, for this is no concern of ours. How can anyone remain long at peace who meddles in other people's affairs; who seeks occasion to gad about, and who makes little or no attempt at recollection? Blessed are the single-hearted, for they shall enjoy much peace.

Thomas à Kempis, *The Imitation of Christ*

Stop intervening in anything which doesn't concern you.

GOD before me, God behind me,
God above me, God below me,
I on the path of God,
God upon my track.
Who is there on the land?
Who is there on wave?
Who is there on billow?
Who is there by doorpost?
Who is there along with us?
God and Lord
I am here abroad,
I am here in need,
I am here in pain,
I am here in straits,
I am here alone,
O God, aid me.
CELTIC PRAYER

🐚 Look around your house, garden or workplace and
imagine Jesus standing in those places, watching over
you. Take solace in this and feel his support, wherever
you are.

Accept that God loves everything

O N one occasion the good Lord said, 'Everything is going to be all right.' On another, 'You will see for yourself that every sort of thing will be all right.' In these two sayings the soul discerns various meanings.

One is that he wants us to know that not only does he care for great and noble things, but equally for little and small, lowly and simple things as well. This is his meaning: '*Everything* will be all right.' We are to know that the least thing will not be forgotten.

ST JULIAN OF NORWICH,
Revelations of Divine Love

🌰 Cut pictures from a newspaper or magazine of prominent people, such as a Prime Minister or President or a member of a Royal Family. Then cut out pictures of less well-known people who, for some reason, are in the news. Add pictures of animals, birds and flowers. Add photographs of yourself and your family. Think of God loving and caring for all those people and creatures. Take comfort that the least thing will not be forgotten by God.

Be risen!

Do you believe that Christ was raised from the dead? Believe the same of yourself. Just as his death is yours, so also is his resurrection; if you have shared in the one, you shall share in the other. As of now sin is done away with.

JOHN CHRYSOSTOM, *Dead to Sin*

🔖 Praise God that you were raised from the dead with him.

Accept you can't do everything by yourself

NOTHING worth doing is completed in our lifetime; therefore we must be saved by hope. Nothing true or beautiful or good makes complete sense in any immediate context of history; therefore we must be saved by faith. Nothing we do, however virtuous, can be accomplished alone, therefore we are saved by love.

REINHOLD NIEBUHR,
The Irony of American History

🕮 Ask God to help you with today's major tasks. Then thank him at the end of the day, whatever the outcome.

Look forward to Jesus' return

THERE will be signs in the sun, the moon, and the stars, and on the earth distress among nations confused by the roaring of the sea and the waves. People will faint from fear and foreboding of what is coming upon the world, for the powers of heaven will be shaken. Then they will see the Son of man coming in a cloud with power and great glory. Now when these things begin to take place, stand up and raise your heads, because your redemption is drawing near.

LUKE 21:25–8

❧ Look forward to Jesus' return to earth, knowing that that will mark the beginning of true peace.

Acknowledgements

My thanks are due to the following people who either directly or indirectly helped me to compile this book: members of the Endowed Mission Hall in Rowley Regis who kindly lent me various spiritual classics; Bruce Clift and Jane Foulkes for introducing me to other useful books; my parents Vera and Richard Round and then-fiancé (now my husband), Grant Filleul who gave me space in which to work; and Christine Smith, editorial director of Marshall Pickering, for her help and encouragement, and for commissioning me in the first place.

The acknowledgements pages constitute an extension of the copyright pages.

Abingdon Press, for excerpts from the following:
1. *Prayer* by George A. Buttrick.
2. *Rule and Exercises of Holy Living* by Jeremy Taylor, from *The Fellowship of the Saints* by Thomas S. Kepler, copyright 1947 by Stone & Peers, copyright renewal 1976 by Florence Tennant Kepler.

Wendy Craig, for an extract from *Show Me the Way*.

Friends United Press, for excerpts from *The Pastoral Letters of George Fox*, edited by T. Canby Jones.

HarperCollins, for excerpts from the following:
1. *The Plain Man's Book of Prayers* by William Barclay.
2. *Approved Unto God* by Oswald Chambers.
3. *Shade of His Hand* by Oswald Chambers.
4. *Shadow of an Agony* by Oswald Chambers.
5. *The Growing Up Pains of Adrian Plass* by Adrian Plass.
6. *With and Without Christ* by Sadhu Sundar Singh.

HarperCollins *Religious*, Melbourne, Australia, for excerpts from *Common Prayer Collection* by Michael Leunig.

Hodder and Stoughton, for excerpts from the following:
1. A *Celebration of Discipline* by Richard Foster.
2. *Finding Freedom* by Joyce Huggett.
3. *The Shattered Lantern* by Ronald Rolheiser.
4. *A Journey Into God* by Delia Smith.

Lutterworth Press, for an excerpt from *Wings of the Morning* by Frank Topping.

Mowbray, for excerpts from *Fat is a Spiritual Issue* by Jo Ind.

Thomas Nelson Inc., for excerpts from *The Imitation of Christ* by Thomas à Kempis, translated by E. M. Blaiklock.

New Reader's Press, for excerpts from *Letters by a*

Modern Mystic by Frank Laubach.

Paulist Press, for excerpts from *The Theologia Germanica of Martyin Luther*, translated by Bengt Hoffman.

Penguin Books, for excerpts from *The Revelation of Divine Love* by Julian of Norwich.

SCM Press, for excerpts from *More Contemporary Prayers* edited by Caryl Micklem.

Sheed & Ward, for an excerpt from *Prayers of Life* by Michel Quoist.

All Bible quotations are taken from the NRSV.